1

Speed Reading the Carousel Way

Stop Reading, Start Visualizing:

The Step-By-Step Process To Fast-Track Your Reading Speed

By Patrick Lightman

Speed Reading the Carousel Way:

Stop Reading, Start Visualizing. The Step-By-Step Process To Fast-Track Your Reading Speed

Discover the SECRET behind SUPERIOR DECISION MAKING:

Click here to grab the CHEAT SHEET.

Table of Contents

Introduction

There are certain skills that we do not really benefit from throughout our lives, and I'm pretty sure one of them is reading.

From the moment our education begins, we are taught to read as part of a process of recognition of symbols, which covers as a layer the verbal expression we give to the objects that surround us.

This is not all bad, but when you are overwhelmed by extreme amounts of text to read, or just feel the need to improve your reading performance, analyzing each word consistently is not only tedious but exhausting, and depending on The pressure you carry on it can end up being frustrating.

How do I know this? I lived it in my own flesh, and by pure coincidence of destiny and some effort on my part, I managed to create an effective solution to end my terrifying reading problem.

Throughout this book, you will get the necessary tools and the right theory to fully understand how the Carousel method really works, because it is so efficient and what you must do to apply it and make the results last over time.

In this way, in the first chapter of the book, I tell you a bit about how my story was, as well as the reasons that pushed me to look for a quick reading method that was easy to understand, learn, practice, and apply for long periods of time without sacrifice neither the speed nor the efficiency of the reading sessions.

Also, in this same chapter I explain in detail how it was that I tried other reading methods, and what were the advantages and disadvantages that I could observe of each of them, including the Israeli method, the skipping method, and some tools that do they proved quite useful when it came to speeding up the process a bit.

Continuing with the story, the second chapter of this book, I explain to you how the "eureka" moment was and how purely coincidental came to me the fundamental principle that I used to create this method while I was wandering in the town fair.

Later, in the third chapter you will find How was the creative process of the Carousel method, as well as the bases on which the two steps that are part of this process are based, giving you to know the evaluation methods necessary to reach a coherent conclusion, what was my initial results, and what key points I had to develop to polish the method that I am giving you.

Also, at this point, I have a first exercise for you to try my Carousel method on your own and you can see the ease of application and the deficiency of its use.

Continuing you will find the necessary knowledge to understand how the cognitive process that you apply when using the Carousel method really works. In this way in the fourth chapter, we talk a little about neuroscience, explaining how the hemispheres of the brain work and how this method makes use of the simplified processes of the right hemisphere that remains always more active in order to speed up the process of receiving information. Additionally, we talked a little about the power of dominance.

And how the dominant hemisphere can influence your reading abilities.

Going forward in the fifth chapter, I explain in detail What is the method of Carousel and exactly how it works, it is at this point that we speak, not of the process, but rather of the final result, the method that I have created and designed based on something of luck, and a deep analysis of the capacities of absorption and handling of the information of our brain.

At this point, we will talk about the strategic objectives of the Carousel method, the skills you put into practice at the moment of using it, and the real difference this method has with traditional reading.

In addition, we briefly go through the fundamental principle of this method and how it works when applied in other disciplines of real life. You will be surprised to learn that the same principle of efficiency that underlies the Carousel method is applied by the engineers who build the space rockets.

Finally, in our final chapter, I have for you a litmus test, a slightly stronger reading designed to show you what has been the improvement in your performance with respect to the moment you started reading the book.

Once you reach that point, you can clearly demonstrate how your reading speed has increased significantly, without sacrificing the understanding you have about the text, much less need two weeks of practice to get to see improvements.

Chapter I: A day in the life of a miserable reader

I know what it feels like to lose, to waste your time as much as your abilities and to feel that the final result Hardly borders on the mediocre. Vera, when I was studying to obtain my master's degree in psychology from the University of Veracruz, I was overwhelmed by the amount of reading we were facing, it was not just any load, any course that I had done before or even after has approached this.

We talked about dozens of essays and readings of books ordered each of the weeks. At first I thought I could easily do this, however it turned out that choosing a master's degree on a subject as broad as clinical psychology under an institution that offers you the title in Just Two Years, implied that all the content that is usually recorded in 4 years of Studies would be delivered to me in half the time.

Well, so I spent the first weeks, unveiling for

hardly meeting the responsibilities assigned to me. For this reason, it does not take long for me to realize that some of my colleagues calmly delivered their essays and always on time, which of course generated a lot of curiosity.

It was a very unusual group, about 5 candidates for masters who only stood out because they were the only ones who were struggling not to fall asleep during the last classes of the night.

Of course, at some point I came to think that they would even be cheating, however everything seemed to be in place, and both the institution and the teachers were too strict to allow this to happen, so I decided to simply follow them day to the library Where they went after school almost every day and ask them exactly what they were doing differently so they could move forward so quickly with the reading of the assigned chapters as well as the papers, and research, and even more important How is it that in such short periods of time they made it so evident that they practically dominated the subjects that we had been assigned to read.

The open path

One of the girls that were part of that group was called Kelly, she was a psychologist who had traveled from Australia to pursue a master's degree in this university, she was a beautiful blonde of 30 years of age with a very professional look and a friendly attitude and relaxed so it was easy enough for me to approach and ask how they were doing exactly to stay in shape with regard to assignments.

- *It is a fairly common method where I come from, although it is of Israeli origin...* - She taught me while offering me a seat at her desk.

The other members of the group had already settled to begin their reading, by that afternoon they would have been programmed to read at least 50 pages, which at first made me feel a little guilty for taking their time that way, however, Kelly began to explain to me what this method was about in a simple way.

After all, it was a learning method that took little more than a few weeks to master moderately, and was also something that coincidentally members of this group already had in common.

That day I felt a stronger frustration than I had before, not only was I struggling to keep up with my assignments, but it could take me weeks or even months to acquire a technique to make my student life easier.

But not everything I was lost, despite the short time I had available I proposed to myself to find an answer to this problem. Clearly, I was already looking for something more concrete than a magical way to deliver my assignments on time, by this point it was already clear what I needed: a way to reduce the time spent reading, without diminishing or risking my ability to reading comprehension.

The failed attempts

So I embarked on the search for a suitable technique and easy to apply or learn to read quickly without having to practice for months or get tangled with complicated mechanisms before you start to see the results.

Of course, the first thing I did was to try to learn the Israeli method quickly, clearly overestimating my self-taught abilities. The fact is that this method requires a high concentration, so you cannot keep it active or read this way for long periods of time which would explain why the boys took the trouble to practice it only once a day and for periods of goals short Additionally, this style of reading was not only tiring, but also quite complicated to apply since it proposed to accelerate your comprehension ability instead of the speed with which you pass the view on the text.

Another method that I had access to is the well-known *skipping*, this method caught my attention because it allowed me to read the books knowing which parts to skip and which parts to focus, but the disadvantages were quite noticeable.

In principle, the first failure of this method was the fact that I lost part of the totally relevant information, additionally although my brain could understand what I was reading without reading it completely get only the essential information meant having knowledge about the structure in which the book was written. So I ended up reading it twice to really understand what was happening with the information and being able to actually store it in my head.

The *skipping* sounds essentially simple since it is about reading the first introductory paragraphs to understand the message of the book and paying special attention to the subtitles and the first and last sentences of each paragraph as well as the one or another keyword to keep the information coherent, but as you can imagine more than 50% of the vital information contained in the text escaped from my hands *-or rather, my eyes-*

Then, despite a few failures, I did manage to get some tips that helped improve my reading ability.

Although I could never really get past the 250 words per minute compared to the 150 words with which I had started my search. So redirect my thoughts to avoid wandering daydreaming, stop subvocalizing what I'm reading, and propose clear reading goals were not enough techniques or at least concise enough to accelerate the process and help me recover those hours of sleep I was losing between work and study.

To sum up

My story begins with the lack of ability to carry all the content of the master's degree in psychology in the necessary time.

Despite obtaining information from my colleagues with better performance, my only great discovery to that point was that "I needed to read faster."

I tried the Israeli method, but it would take too

long to be mastered and demand a high level of concentration, so I could not use it for long study sessions.

The method of Skipping was much lighter, however, it involved sacrificing enormously the reception of information

Other techniques to improve reading performance were useful, but I saw no real significant improvements.

The answer remained a mystery.

Chapter II: A not-so-monumental discovery at a fun fair

Incredibly, and in a somewhat frustrating way I must add, some months had already passed during which I was still facing a pretty mediocre performance.

It was already mid-August, and the summer in the place was quite warm Although in the afternoon the trees of the grounds around where my room was rented caused a sensation of freshness that had attracted me there every time I felt suffocated.

The moment in which "it" came to me was neither Exact nor something that I expected.

A day at the fair

It was a Saturday around 6 o'clock in the afternoon, I was overwhelmingly tired, I felt my eyelids heavy and honestly I could not focus on a single task without stopping to think about everything else that I had to be doing also at that moment. *-And to all this stress, I had to add music from the fair that had been installed in the nearby land.*

I wanted to take a break from work and rest for a while in my bed, but something between the music, the smells of food, and the laughter of the people was just irritating me.

-Looking at it in retrospect, I think at that moment all I felt was envy for all those people who were out relaxed enjoying the fair drinking beer at and eating junk food while having a good time with their friends or family.

In conclusion, I did not have the strength or motivation to continue working, and external agents seemed too tempting to give up sleeping.

So I decided to go out and clear my mind like I did when the fair was not on the ground.

I dressed up the best I could. Even though it was a fair in the open field I did not want to meet any of my colleagues and let it be so obvious that I was physically devastated by the workload.

So, I took my leather jacket and made sure there was enough money inside to at least take a couple of beers and buy myself something to eat.

The place looked extremely different from what it was normally. Instead of a partially open field, covered with trees sufficiently distanced so that one could rest without having so many people nearby and give out a fresh but clear environment, I found a space completely crammed with gaming machines and stalls. It turns out that the smells of the food that came to my room were the mixture of at least a dozen different stalls, each offering a different kind of junk food, and arranged on the right-hand side in the great hallway that all the stalls had formed at the entrance of the fair.

-Now I also have to choose carefully what I'm going to eat - I thought as I prepared to enter the place.

In my discouragement, I decided to go directly to a small liquor stand near the wider land clearing. - They had arranged a platform in this space, in which there was a small band playing covers of The Beatles while the crowd was distributed along attractions that formed a circle starting from that platform and leaving the clear space enclosed so that children did not run towards the forest.

It was a craft beer stand, staffed by two very nice girls, both distinctly of German origin. There were quite a few options to choose from, but since I had time without knowing what the sea was like, I got carried away by nostalgia and bought a jar of coconut beer.

They gave me a huge wooden jar, which would

have at least one liter of capacity and was filled to the brim; to my surprise it was extremely tasty, so I bought a few pretzels with cheese in the same place to have something salty to accompany it with and I drank almost half jar with a single blow.

Eureka

So, there I was, tired, annoyed, and sitting alone on a bench in the park watching as people passed by enjoying the afternoon while I was absorbed in my dilemma using a rather sweet beer and a few snacks as a lifesaver when the Beatles tribute band got off the stage and an original band that was apparently famous in town went on to play. It was still a soft Rock, but it was much more rhythmic and easier to enjoy for me.

Just at that moment, most parts of the people who were watered by the place was concentrating just in front of the stage, and that's when I saw it.

Right there I found myself watching the Carousel

on the other side of the park, it was quite far from me and I was already going through the third liter of beer, so it was a little difficult for me to focus on one far away target at the time, first I only saw some colors going around, which made me a little dizzy; for When I focus the view a second time I could denote the dolls that were in the Carousel and which had people mounted and which were not; the third time I focused my eyes on the Carousel I was surprised that I could notice more details, like the kind of people mounted on each of the dolls; for example, there was a small child with straight black hair mounted on a small red Ford Mustang model, A girl around 16 years old was in one of the planes and in the other two that were close to her, there was another young man about the same age and another girl who kept shouting things to the first, so I could quickly assume that they went to the fair together

By taking a fourth look at the Carousel, I could see even more details about them. It was then when it hit me! I could use this method of image perception in the brain to speed up my reading performance, I just had to find a way to replace the more visible, moderately visible and less visible groupings of characteristics, with similar groups of text.

Thank God I had a pencil in my jacket and some paper in my wallet to take not of the idea, even when for a moment I was tempted to discard it, because I was not far from the level of drunkenness you are in when you think that maybe you could throw everything overboard and go to get a very spontaneous tattoo. But the next day I would put the idea to the test and the results would really surprise me.

To sum up

During what we might consider a dark moment, my place of relaxation was interrupted by the town fair.

Maybe it would be the beer, or maybe the

tiredness, but when the crowd opened my eyes to observe the carousel of the fair in the distance, the first general concept of my new writing method came to life.

The accuracy in which I saw the images of the carousel, increasing with each round seemed to be the key, or at least that's what I felt

I had the idea, but the structure was missing. Could it work?

Chapter III: A small step for a Brainiac, a giant leap for ME

I was not so lost any more since I had an idea about how to improve my performance that maybe could take me further faster than the other options that had been presented to me so far could do so.

Of course, in this chapter, we are going to talk about exactly this, how I converted the crazy idea of adapting my visualization method in a drunken moment to what would now be a complete and totally efficient reading method.

The day after the fair I took a pencil and paper, and I set out to structure ways in which I could apply this method to start practicing it as soon as possible. The first thing I did was to establish the key points:

Visually, the first thing is to adapt the eyes

This is quite easy when it comes to a Carousel, a painting, a landscape or even any other composite object; however, when dealing with text it is a little more difficult since all the written words have to do exactly the same size and with the same degree of pressure in the ink.

This is where the procedure started to fork, on the one hand, I thought about adopting a bit of the quick reading methods I had previously achieved, focusing only on the first paragraphs of the content, the last paragraph, and some keywords.

But far above convenient, adding all this information to the first round of the text Carousel became a long process.

The second option that I planted at that time was simply to look over the text as you do when you first see the Carousel, and in the same way, only process the information that jumps into view. The detail with this part of the process is that normally our eyes more easily detect words that have been emphasized, those that are surrounded by commas, or those that are well known to us. For this reason, I concluded that the most efficient would be to mix both processes.

In conclusion, the step 1 of my Carousel method for quick reading is "looking over the text" in a somewhat loose way trying to concentrate only in the obvious keywords that may exist in the content.

This way, if for example you are trying to quickly read a book on how to make cakes, you should clearly think that there are obvious words like *cake, flour or mix*, which are distributed around the text and that can help you establish a base of information to which you will be adding the content in the following rounds.

To continue, it was not only about reading but about doing it at a time when it is efficient.

For this reason, I had to compare my usual reading time by applying the tools I already knew to be able to define a time in which I felt there really was an improvement significant enough to consider the experiment a success.

To make a comparison what I did was to choose a couple of academic texts of approximately the same length and to apply in the first place the first tips that I had achieved when reading the first text.

Considering that both texts were around 500 words, that is to say, that they were quite short, I realized that I was able to capture the important information in an approximate time of 2 and a half minutes, which was quite on par with my Previous times (that is, 250 words per minute)

For the second block of text, I applied only the first reading, so I only passed the view on the text processing only the most outstanding words and focusing especially on the basic keywords of the content.

Reading this way the five hundred words of the second block of text did not take me more than 10 seconds, however, it does not absorb the necessary information so as to be able to make judgments about what existed or not within that content.

Clearly, he had to find a way to absorb more information in the first visualization of the text or simply to proceed as a second round.

So then I carefully designed the second round of my Reading Carousel.

As when I visualized the Carousel at the fair, at this point, I repeated the process of the first visualization but allowing me to observe in more detail the groups of words that surrounded the main keywords and the most visible ones that found during the first round.

This second reading took me a little more than a minute, but what is important here, is that I realized that I understood much more of the text without needing to dig too much into it.

I could also notice that when observing the text as an image looking for groups of words around the keywords, and the words highlighted after the first visualization, the focus was unexpectedly focused on groups of three to four words mostly.

This last detail has a certain logic because if we think about it carefully the process is the same as when we proceed with a visual object, be it an art piece or some examples that we have named above.

That is, I was successfully managing to see instead of reading the text and understanding the information without the need for posterior analysis.

So far the experiment seemed a success, I had managed to observe the text of 500 words, exhausting a basically minimal amount of time between 80 and 90 seconds, and fully understanding a large part of the information obtained from the text.

But all this still had to discard all the problems with which I had found when applying the other methods. A clear example is that of the Iran method and that requires a high level of concentration, which is why sight quickly gets tired.

So I had to analyze what I was doing a little more thoroughly in order to qualify my new idea as an efficient and appropriate reading method

The evaluation process

By comparing my method with the methods with which I failed earlier I realized that I was avoiding certain problems easily.

To begin with, compared to the Israeli method, it does not involve suffering from any type of exhaustion, since when observing instead of reading, the sight gets much less tired and I have seen, with some practice, the ability to read up to 30000 words in a single session without feeling so exhausted.

Since the Israeli method requires a high level of concentration could not be applied for such long periods of time, to this we must add the fact that it takes a few weeks to implement this method efficiently.

Something that did catch my attention is the fact that I was not sacrificing comprehension of the text when I reduced the reading time, when doing a more exhaustive analysis, I understood that it was the way in which my brain was processing the information I was offering him because of the change in the method of inserting or receiving this information. But we will talk about this a bit later.

Another method with which I tried before was skipping, which as I explained it is about skipping part of the text and focus only on keywords and the first last paragraphs of each section.

Unlike the skipping method, what I learned with the Carousel of the fair did not mean skipping the whole body of the text, so I was able to absorb practically all the important information without sacrificing more time or paying extra attention to reading.

Even though skipping is a bit like what I was doing, which to be honest generated certain doubts at the beginning, it turns out that I try to oblige my brain to process information in a different way, converting it into images and artistic analysis those items that we normally see as language analysis.

Additionally, other tips that I got to read faster such as silencing your internal voice at the time of reading, setting clear goals for reading turned out to be additional tools instead of methods by themselves, and are perfectly applicable in conjunction with the Carousel method.

What my brain got

Here begins the surprising part of all this.

As I mentioned before, the difference between this form of reading and any of the traditional forms or the methods that I could find to speed up reading as such lies directly in the perception with which we are entering information into the brain.

Normally to read what we do it is to ingest words, in other words, with the sight we are absorbing pre-established codes based on our knowledge of the language. Then our brain processes these codes as it would do if they were mathematical codes, providing us with meaning based on what we know what those codes mean and therefore resulting in a complex use of our cognitive capacity.

On the contrary, the method I discovered that night staring at the Carousel, and developed later, focuses more on using the artistic side of the brain, that is, how we handle images as images and not as codes of encrypted information.

To put it differently, normally if you see an apple, you think of apple as a word. Similarly, when reading the word apple, you think of an apple as an item *—And you surely just did imagine an apple, didn't you?*

In this same way when you see the text instead of reading it and analyzing it with your mind, your brain automatically has the ability to create the concept without the need for analysis.

This is done through the artistic part of your brain, the visual effects away from logic and language are usually processed with the right hemisphere, and so even if you find it more difficult at first the thought process, you will notice that underlying process the information faster unconsciously.

About this, there are certain key points to take into account. First of all, given that the left side of the brain dominates the cognitive processes linked to language, as well as the more complex thought processes, it can be a bit difficult to turn off this process of analysis to simply observe how you would do with your natural environment or how a piece of art that you normally process as language codes.

Another very interesting key point is that people like me whose right hemisphere is dominant, train this technique more quickly, while people whose dominant hemisphere is the left one (right-handed people) would have to practice once or twice to start seeing results.

If you want to break your mind's paradigm of processing the left hemisphere information through reading, a simple exercise you can do is read the text upside down.

You see, we usually read from left to right, and this we do because of our brain's need to analyze information in that order to capture it quickly.

There are examples of languages such as Chinese or Japanese that are read in different directions from top to bottom, or right to left, which is why their cognitive systems are more varied and have, in general, a broader perception of language than ours.

Remember that language is no more than symbols, arranged by us to represent objects, situations or entities that we already visualize with our eyes or analyze with the rest of our senses.

Going back to the example of the apple, when you look at one you do not necessarily do it from right to left regardless of whether you are right-handed or left-handed. On the contrary, normally when we visualize something with the intention of analyzing it, we do it from the top down or from the bottom up, which is exactly what you are going to do in the first step of this method to analyze the content of the text without having to actually read it.

All images, no text

Just as young children are educated with picture books instead of text, and little by little words and language are added to their education, it is easy to understand how to use sight to process written information instead of performing an analysis of reading generates an informative understanding easier to process.

During the time I was developing this method to speed reading, I realized that my mind was throwing more concrete images and more often than when I just read quickly using traditional reading methods.

To put it in a simpler way, when I read fast, I throw one image at a time to remind me of the real meaning of what I am reading, while through the Carousel method that I was developing, the images came before the understanding. It was made easier thanks to the memories in my mind of the images contained in the code of words to understand the words' information.

Basically, our brain does all the work in automatic processing the words as images so that we can consciously turn those images into information and analyze it.

It's already time for you to try my theory

At this moment I will have a small 500-word text for you, quite similar in length to the ones I use to try out the method for the first time.

The text that you see below is public content, and I invite you to keep track of the time it takes to read it using the Carousel method.

Remember that what you are going to do is to perform the first two basic rounds of the Carousel method that I have designed, that is:

1. Fly your eyes through the text searching for keywords or words that stand out easily in your eyes.

2. Recalling the words you previously obtained, re-visualize the text from top to bottom, carefully observing groups of words housed in conjunction with the words you could observe during the first round.

If you are ready, proceed with the text:

A SCANDAL IN BOHEMIA

From The Adventures of Sherlock Holmes by Arthur Conan Doyle

For him, she was always the woman. In fact, I could hardly remember seeing him refer to her in any other way. From his perspective, she eclipsed everything with her sex and it was not as if he felt any clue of love for Irene Adler. Any emotion like this was an aberration to his cold, stable, and perfectly balanced mind. Holmes was a calm man and was undoubtedly the most perfect machine of reasoning and observation in history, however, as a lover, he lacked the skills to always be in the right position and could find himself in blackspots every now and then. He never spoke about these passions unless he did it in a mocking tone. These were things worth observing, perfect for investigating the motives and actions of men. But for him as a trained researcher and reasoner, letting such emotions enter his sensitive and balanced mental equilibrium would only bring doubt, causing problems to all his deductions and the structure that follows. As a break in a sensitive instrument, or A crack in the surface of a powerful lens, it could be disturbing, the presence of these feelings, in nature as strange as his. And yet there was only one woman in his mind, and it was the late Irene Adler of dubious memory.

I've seen little of him lately. My marriage had caused a distance between us. My interested in establishing my home life, and all the responsibilities that arise around a man who enjoys complete happiness were enough to keep all my attention focused, while he, who was moving away from any form of society with all his energy, continued to settle down in our old lodgings on Baker Street, consuming information from his old books and alternating his experiences between cocaine and ambition, the forced stupor of the drug and the accurate and relentless energy of his own nature.

Holmes remained as always, fervently attracted to the study of crime and applying ordinary powers of observation and cognitive deduction skills to follow the clues and clear up those mysteries that official institutions had left behind after the failure to discover the truth. Every so often, I heard whispers or received vaguely informed news of his actions: his summons to Odessa during Trepoff's case, his participation in the tragedy of the Atkinson and Trincomalee brothers, and the mission that he would have carried out successfully for the real family of Holland. However, above these small indicators of his activity, which I simply shared with my readers on the newspaper, there was little I knew about my old friend and companion.

On March 20, 1888, returning from a trip of a patient (after rejoining the civil practice) I went on course Baker Street. When I passed that night by our door, that which my mind associates with my courtship and the tragic incidents of Study In Scarlet, I felt the immense desire to see Holmes

Maybe it seems hard to believe but as you may have noticed it is quite easy to capture the information by using this process, and you also manage to spend a much shorter timespan than you usually would.

This is how I learnt that great discoveries arrive when we least expect it, whether it's an apple falling in your lap or a first blurry look at the Carousel of the town fair after you've had a few beers, what exactly allowed me to find the way to use the artistic analysis of the right side of the brain to leave in your hands today a new and excellent reading tool, which will later explain exactly how it works.

In this third chapter, we cover a good amount of information, you already have an idea of how I discovered how to adapt our artistic cognitive process to the analysis of information through language symbols which are normally part of the more complex information analysis process of the brain.

Additionally you could observe what are the advantages I got from this process compared to the methods I had previously found, both based on the time it took to analyze the reading, as well as the time I can apply to use the method and even more important the quality with which I perceive and keep the information in my brain after reading and got the chance to try it out, which must have taken around 1 minute or 1:20 minutes at the first try.

To sum up

I already had an idea of the principle I was going to apply to create the Carousel method, but I still needed to establish the exact processes to convert an environment visualization process into a reading process.

The key points of the process are to focus on the

most visible objects during the first round and to deepen the focus during the second round.

My first option was to apply part of the skipping method, but when taking full paragraphs for the first reading it was impossible not to generate an analysis which hinders the measurement of time.

The second option consisted of simply seeing the text from top to bottom as if they were images, leaving the most important words to be visible.

In this way, the first step of the Carousel method was to observe the text in a lazy way, giving a simple approach to the keywords and the occasional word that appears without needing to pay more attention.

After several exercises conclude this first round should take about 10 seconds for every 500 words, but it was not enough to reach a conclusion regarding the content of the text.

In order to absorb the information in a concrete way, I dedicated myself to observe the same previous keywords but taking into account their environment as I did with the Carousel.

This second reading I take the beginning about a minute.

As a result, the first attempts offered me a performance of 90 seconds for every five hundred words.

I could evaluate the practice of this method incisions of up to 3000 words, with what I discovered that it does not cause so much eyestrain since it requires low levels of concentration.

Additionally, I could evaluate the way in which the information was processed by my brain, and specifically understand that I was absorbing the necessary information without needing to pay so much attention to the text.

Testing the exercise you will have realized what it takes much less time to perform the reading with the method of Carousel, although it is possible that the first time did not absorb all the information in the way expected, this improves more and more with practice.

Chapter IV: A little bit of neuroscience

A creative person is one who can process the information available, the sensory data that we all receive, and make something new with it.

In this way, a musician needs notes, a writer needs words, a painter needs visual insights, and all of them need some knowledge of the necessary techniques to transform that raw material information into something new and amazing.

About this, many creative people have recognized the differences between the two processes: collecting data and transforming them creatively, and recent findings of brain functioning begin to clarify this dual process.

What does this have anything to do with us?

Well, to begin with, the carousel process that I developed requires you to use both sides of your brain, but especially your right hemisphere.

For this reason, we dedicated this chapter to review some recent important discoveries on the field of neuroscience, which had greatly expanded scientific theories about the nature of human consciousness and are deeply linked to how you can improve your reading process through this method.

Know both sides of your brain

Seen from above, the human brain recalls the appearance of a tasty walnut. It has two rounded halves, with a convoluted surface connected by the center.

These two halves are called ***"left hemisphere"*** and ***"right hemisphere"***. In this regard, our nervous system is connected to the brain through a cross connection, so that the right hemisphere controls the left side of the body, and the left hemisphere controls the right side.

Also, given to this crossing of the nerve pathways, your left hand is controlled by the right hemisphere, and your right hand by the left hemisphere.

This works in the same way for animals, whose two hemispheres are essentially the same or symmetric in their functions.

However, the human hemispheres present a functional asymmetry which most notorious effect is the predominance of the use of one hand over the other.

Over the past 150 years, scientists have known that the function of language and language-related abilities are located in the left hemisphere for most humans.

The language and the words are closely linked with the reasoned thought and with the other elevated mental functions that distinguish us from other creatures, and for that reason, scientists considered that the left hemisphere was the dominant one, and the right the subordinate.

The general opinion, which prevailed until very recently, was that the right half of the brain was less advanced, less evolved than the left half; a kind of twin of inferior capacity, directed and maintained by the left hemisphere, the verbal one.

An interesting fact is that neurologists were intrigued by the functions of a thick nervous cable, made up of millions of fibers that connect the two brain hemispheres.

This connection cable, the corpus callosum had all the appearance of being an important structure, given its large size, the enormous number of nerve fibers that compose it, and its strategic location as a connector between the two hemispheres but all evidence indicated that it could be completely cut off without producing major effects.

In the '50s, some studies run by Roger W. Sperry, Ronald Myers, Colwyn Trevarthen and other collaborators at the California Institute of Technology, established that an important function of the corpus callosum was to communicate the two hemispheres, allowing the transmission of memory and learning. It was found that if the connection was surgically cut, the two halves continued to function independently, which partly explained the apparent lack of effect on behavior and functioning.

In the next decades, similar studies were conducted with human patients, showing that, for real, both hemispheres intervene in high cognitive functions, although each half of the brain is specialized, in a complementary way, in different forms of thought, both very complex.

Since this new concept of the brain has important implications for education in general, and for learning to draw, read and write in particular, I will briefly describe some of the research known as the "divided brain studies".

The investigation focused on a small group of individuals who were severely disabled by epileptic disorders that affected both hemispheres, and whose transmission of attacks between the two hemispheres was cutting the corpus callosum and the adjacent commissures, after all the other measures failed, thus isolating each hemisphere of the other.

The operation had the expected result: the attacks were controlled and the patients recovered their health. Despite the radical nature of the operation, it seems that the patients did not see their external appearance, movements, and coordination altered.

And for a casual observer, their daily behavior did not change much either.

> *"The main issue is that there seem to be two ways of thinking, verbal and non-verbal, represented respectively by the left hemisphere and the right and that our educational system, as well as science in general, tends to despise the non-verbal form of the intellect. The result is that modern society manifests discrimination against the right hemisphere" (Roger W. Sperry, 1974)*

Thereafter, the team from the California Institute of Technology worked with these patients in a series of tests that revealed the separate functions of the two hemispheres showing that each hemisphere, in a certain sense, perceives reality in his own way.

The verbal half of the brain - the left hemisphere - dominates most of the time in individuals with intact brains. This also happened in patients with a divided brain; however, through ingenious procedures, the scientists studied the functioning of the right half of the patients' brain, discovering that this non-verbal half also receives sensations, responds with feelings and processes information on its own.

In a brain with intact Corpus callosum, hemispheric communication fuses or reconciles the two types of perception, thus maintaining our sense of being "a person," a unitary being.

> *"The data indicate that the non-verbal hemisphere is specialized in global perception, synthesizing the information that comes to it. The verbal and dominant hemisphere, on the other hand, seems to work in a more logical and analytical way. Its language is inadequate for the fast and complicated synthesis that the subordinate hemisphere performs"* *(Jerre Levy and Roger. W. Sperry, 1968)*

The evidence of the studies showed that the left

hemisphere mode of processing information is verbal and analytical, while the right hemisphere is nonverbal and global. Subsequently, Jerre Levy discovered that the processing in the right hemisphere is rapid, complex, totalizing, spatial and perceptive and that this processing is not only different but of complexity comparable to that of the verbal and analytical mode of the left hemisphere. –Even more interesting, they concluded that the two types of processing tended to interfere with each other, preventing maximum performance which explains why evolution separated both processes in different hemispheres-

To sum up, both hemispheres use high-level modes of cognition, which, although different, involve thinking, reasoning, and complicated mental functioning. And as a result of these amazing discoveries, we now know that even though we continue to feel a single being, our brains are double, and each half has its own form of knowledge and its own way of perceiving reality.

What are the brain hemispheres?

To put it simply, our brain is made up of two halves, the right half is known as the right hemisphere and the left one as the left hemisphere.

Each hemisphere is dedicated to different functions, for which one of the fundamental features of the cerebral structure is the functional variance that exist between both of them.

In addition it has been demonstrated that each of them is focused in the development of different behaviors.

It is also convenient to know that there is an inverted relationship between both sides of the brain and our body.

In this regard, the right hemisphere is responsible for managing and controlling the movement of the left part of our body, while the left hemisphere coordinates the right one.

The right hemisphere

It is demonstrated that spatial discernment, orientation, emotional behavior, the faculty to control the nonverbal traits of communication, instinct, recognition, and memory of faces, sounds and voices, are located in this side of the brain.

In addition, there is an important aspect to our learning method, the right brain develops its processes in images.

Various studies have shown that people whose dominant hemisphere is the right one tend to study, think, remember and learn in images which allows them to have an extra kick in creative and imaginative tasks.

The left hemisphere

On the other hand, the left half is more complex, and is related to the verbal part of our behavior and communication.

In addition to the verbal function, the left side of

our brain has other functions such as analysis, and logical reasoning.

In this regard, people whose dominant hemisphere is the left one –That is right handed people- have a better time communicating and solving numerical problems as well as processing logical information.

The power of dominance

After years of studies, most experts agree that the left hemisphere is by far the most dominant one, and in consequence it has been the one submitted to most studies.

In this regard, hemisphere dominance does play part on the development of each individual, but this does not mean that a person whose right hemisphere is dominant can't exceed in left-oriented activities or the other way around.

To sum up

A creative person processes the information and

turns it into something new

The process by which your brain converts the information you read into knowledge works just like any other creative process, comparable to what an engineer, painter, or architect does when they create their works.

Your brain is divided into two parts, a right hemisphere, and a left hemisphere.

Your right shoulder controls the left part of your body and takes care of the basic processes so that it handles information faster than the left hemisphere.

On the other hand, the left hemisphere is responsible for the deepest cognitive development, including the relationship of symbols derived in language and physical functions relative to the right side of your body.

Each of the hemispheres fulfills different functions and handles fundamental aspects for the organization and function of your body.

In each person there is a dominant hemisphere, which is normally perceptible through the hand that is used more frequently, that is if it is left-handed or right-handed.

People whose right hemisphere has more control over the functions, have to have a facility for creative and artistic development, so if you are one of them the method of Carousel will be much easier.

Chapter V: The Carousel Method

So far, I've already brought you up to date on how I came to the conclusion of creating the Carousel method. However, we are going to dedicate this chapter to open step by step so that you understand in a much more efficient way how the method works and how you are going to apply it.

To begin it is important to know that the method of Carousel to read quickly that we have worked so far is based mainly on the ability we have to use the artistic side of the brain, aka your right hemisphere, to understand the information presented in the text as if they were images.

It is important that you consider it in the following way, your brain is responsible for all the cognitive processes to which your senses submit, in this way the right side of the brain that is known as the artistic side, performs by default the simpler functions, while the left side deals with the complex functions related to logic, indirect analysis and information, and cognitive functions more aligned to what is language and the use of symbols and encryption.

By understanding this you can take into account the following, your brain is actually two brains as we have explained in chapter 4, therefore, in reality, all the information you are processing constantly process it twice.

In this way, while the left side of the brain analyzes in a more profound way all the information it perceives, the right side takes care of the most subtle perceptions, and in all cases, the information received through your senses to bounce between hemispheres, generating between them a feedback that later becomes the logical result obtained.

What we achieved through the Carousel method, is to open the perception of the information contained in the text through the right side of the brain, and therefore achieving a faster absorption of the basic information contained in the symbols, that is to say in the words, making use of the connections previously established in your memory between words and the realities they represent.

With this we achieve two objectives:

- The first is that by not focusing directly on the text and analyzing it constantly you can read more quickly while you wear less your sight.

- The second objective that we achieve thanks to this method is that your brain automatically analyzes the pre-established images based on your prior knowledge of the language.

The skills

At first it seems quite simple the way in which the Carousel method that you are learning through this book is applied, however, there are a number of skills that you are constantly developing without realizing it and mainly one of these is the one you allows you to use this method to speed up your reading speed.

The ability we are talking about is processing information, this skill is what sculptors, painters, and engineers use, as well as anyone who is willing to create something by using any available resource and knowledge about that resource with the purpose of creating something new.

Precisely that is what the learning processes are about, to start it is important that you know how to speak and read the language in which you are applying this method if you want to be able to obtain the results.

The reason is quite simple, once you know the

language you have the basic knowledge of what each of the words means and what the interlaced word sets mean, which later allows your brain to process the information to reach a conclusion.

This conclusion to which your brain has come after the cognitive process of receiving and processing information is exactly the same as a painter does when he takes brushes and paints to capture a picture on a canvas.

Only that, in this case, the process is much simpler. First, replace the canvas for the space provided for new knowledge in your brain, and then change what would be the raw materials for the information you are getting through your senses.

In this way the reading process changes drastically, since you are not processing information slowly, but you get it quickly through the images of the words instead of the words directly and in this way we take advantage of the ability to your brain to maintain the knowledge about the meaning of the words that are in the text thanks to the previous learning that you have on the language.

How is this different from traditional reading?

The difference in terms of the process with respect to normal reading or any other reading technique that we have spoken through the book is that by applying the Carousel technique we are changing the way in which it obtains the raw material, "the words".

The traditional reading method that you were taught at school would be as if the painter had to go to make the paintings to start painting on the canvas, in that case, your brain takes the words to generate an image (the meaning of the word) and after generating the image, it processes the information.

On the contrary, through this method, the right side of your brain takes the words directly to the images, which means that you will not consciously think of transforming the word into an image, in this way your brain makes a part of it free of the work and you can advance faster with your reading efficiently processing the information captured in the text.

The root of the problem is education

With a little more research I came to understand that the root of my problem was based on my previous education.

You will see from small when they teach us to read everything starts well. They teach us words based on images when we learn to speak, and later they teach us that those words can be expressed in other images, through written symbols.

Do you know how "learning" works?

At some point it is normal to ask yourself these key questions about learning:

- Why some people cannot apply the theoretical information learned?

- Why are attention rates so varied from person to person when viewing the same object?

- What makes retention more or less effective in an individual?

After years of research, most students of the subject on cognitive development and the learning process establish that there are certain principles that apply to the educational process and that allow or not the formation of knowledge in the database of the individual.

These principles, work in unison during the real learning experiences of each individual and are functionally inseparable

Prior knowledge can help or may hinder learning

There are cases in which learning is hampered by the inability of the receiver to absorb new knowledge, especially if it collides with the principles that already have patterned within their belief scheme.

In the case of the carousel method that I offer in this book, prior knowledge is a tool, since the database that previously exists in your memory on the use of language, plays a key role to speed up your reading: it works as a bridge between the visual symbols of the text and the recognition of reality by your mind.

The way knowledge is organized influences learning and its application

In a natural way, your mind allows you to create connections between pieces of information.

When those connections form precise knowledge structures and organized with meaning, you will improve your ability to recover and apply this knowledge effectively.

In this way, the wider your vocabulary and the more accurate your knowledge of grammar and spelling, the easier it is for your brain to use the carousel method to connect information quickly.

Targeted practice improves the quality of learning

Learning and performance are encouraged when practices with a clear focus based on specific objectives or criteria.

In other words, when the level of challenge is appropriate and when its amount and frequency are sufficient, it is easier for you to achieve constant improvements with respect to your previous reading speed.

To be self-taught, you must learn to measure and adjust your approaches to learning

Another determining factor in the learning process is the ability to learn on their own.

It is likely that you already have this ability to some degree, which is why you are reading this book instead of looking for a face-to-face course. However, the way you get involved with the goal-setting process is the first major factor in how successful your foray into just a new topic is - whether you're looking for the ability to read faster or the techniques essential for making cakes.

After taking these principles into account, I want you to understand more directly how your normal learning process works.

According to Piaget (1958), who established the most supported theory so far, the theory of cognitive development, a learning process consists of two phases:

- **Assimilation**: In which what is perceived

in the external world is incorporated into the internal world, without changing the structure of that internal world

- **Accommodation**: in which the internal world has to accommodate the external evidence with which it faces

In comparison, these two phases are identified at the time of reading by traditional methods, but also when establishing new knowledge through the carousel method that I teach in this book.

The usual reading process

When we are educated as kids a cycle is created, because when we are taught to read, the first images that we obtained as part of the knowledge about the world that surrounds us are put aside and to have a perception about reality our brain transforms the symbols into words and words in pictures.

This way, the process of recognition of information

embodied in any text becomes a three-step process when it could well be two.

Now let's take a look at the bigger picture here, keep in mind that these three steps happen once per word and then once for each set of words that has additional meaning.

Returning to the example that places you in chapter 3, if you read the word "apple" you think of the image of an apple.

At this time your brain has done all three steps, took the symbols that make up the word apple in the text, created the word apple in your mind, and then turned it into the image of an apple.

As you probably have understood, this happens with a single word, which means that if you read 500 words like the one I had for you as an introductory exercise in chapter 3, this process is repeating 500 times right?

Well, the truth is that no, because it also happens that your brain processes groups of words with added meanings.

If for example, you read the phrase "the apple is on the table" your brain repeats the process for the keywords, "apple, is, table" and generates a new image based on the situation created with this set of words.

If we take into account that each phrase is created by a set an average of 4 words, in a text of 500 words you would be processing around 125 sets of words.

All this for a brand new total of 625 processes approximately for a text of less than one page.

By this, we mean that your brain is doing a 3 step process 625 times, for a total of 1875 steps.

Nevertheless, even when it is practically impossible to reduce these steps to half or less, through the Carousel method we get rid of the most complicated step for the brain, which is to process the word and turn it into an image.

The right hemisphere of your brain is responsible for more artistic work than the left and therefore allows you to directly visualize the image through the text without having to process it as a word, say without processing it as symbols attached to a meaning, but rather as the graphic representation of a direct image.

In this way, we can define that the mistake made in our basic education, lies mainly in forcing the reading process through exercises to read faster with the guidance of a pencil or a rule, or even using your internal voice, which actually makes you read slowly to better understand the text.

The Carousel Method

The method we describe in this book consists of a finger-step structure based on two techniques designed with the intention of making the most of your brain's basic visual perception and the development of your learning process.

The first step is the technique of passing the view over the text, this should be done quickly and lightly, without focusing much of the view except for keywords that you might already be looking for, or words in the case highlighted by the text that you cannot avoid to be seen.

What you are going to do in this step, is to treat the entire text as if it were a soup of letters, as well as those that come in the newspaper.

That is, the text from top to bottom, bottom to top, or from one side to the other as you are more comfortable, and shortly you will find the most important keywords based on the main topic covered in the text.

Once this is done you will have obtained general ideas about the content, such as the main idea, the structure of the text block you are reading, and some general orders, how specific words would help you form an idea of what the text is about.

The second technique consists of its own part in

reviewing the text again, but this time in a slightly calmer way and paying attention to existing blocks or sets of words that form short sentences, these phrases contain more specific information, which will allow you to easily get a clear idea of the most relevant information in the text as well as probably the root of the reasoning behind what is written.

For this second round, it is important that you become aware of the additional information such as images. That is to say, that he observes them is like an outline around the keyword that you could observe in the first round.

Remember that the important thing of this exercise is to consider the text as images in such a way that our brain evaluates and processes the text directly in images, as it would do when we observe our surroundings.

In this way, the first technique is directed to what you see for example the apple, while in the second round you can show your surroundings, in this case, keeping the same example above, series the table and any other object that is around.

As you can see, the most important thing of this exercise is to allow your brain to process the information of words as images automatically, which you can achieve simply by reading quickly without repeating the words constantly in your mind.

What I try to tell you with this is that you turn off your conscious process of collecting information and allow your brain to act automatically to connect the symbols directly with the images without connecting them with the meaning in words, a process that occurs unconsciously.

From the carousel to fast reading

Do you remember when I told you at the beginning of the book the story about how I came to this technique? Well, the connection is quite simple, a Carousel tour offers you a mandatory linear view of a part of the object, so you cannot observe it as a whole at any time.

The same happens with the film tapes, we observe an image at the same time which allows us to analyze the subconsciously more easily than we do with the text.

You may have noticed this before, it is easier to memorize the dialogues of a movie or to remember exactly what happened in each scene, than to open a textbook and be fully prepared for an exam.

While we normally blame the entertainment factor for our index of attention, the truth is that the brain processes images as knowledge automatically, while the text must be analyzed and compared with the images of reality to finally have a meaning in our mind.

> *The existing principles that make up this method of reading, derive directly from the Carousel.*

When you observe a Carousel, as I mentioned

earlier you observe only one part at a time, and you can hardly observe every detail automatically because of the movement.

On the other hand, as the Carousel goes around and repeating the images, you have an increasingly clear perception of what is in it.

In a first round a simple perception of the colors and shapes that make up the games of the Carousel, if you have good eyesight, you could even people who are mounted in each of the games, but you would never get a specific or detailed perception of each one of them, neither of the games nor of the people.

Then, as the second round comes, your perception of the images you received previously improves, allowing you to observe more details of each of the objects present in the Carousel.

You could denote the details of the figures that make up the game, whether they are airplanes or vehicles arranged for people to ride.

Additionally, your brain could process a new and greater amount of details of the people who are in it. Details such as hair color, skin color, clothes they wear, build, and even an approximate age.

The second lesson

This is the second lesson we want to teach you in this book.

You see, it is quite important that you understand that by having two steps in this process what we are doing is building a system, which, like any system or production process, is established from highest to lowest, generating a panoramic view of the information, then establish more specific achievements.

In other words, we start with an overview of the content and then proceed to analyze the details.

This procedure also exists in each and every one of the creative processes.

A clear example would be a painting. At the moment of painting a painting, the artist first establishes the bases, creating contours and shadows which will serve to frame as an environment the images that star in his work.

In this way, if it were the painting of an apple on a table, the painter would work first in the background, then on the table, and finally in the block.

Although we take these objects in the opposite order when practicing the Carousel method to speed up reading, the basic principle is the same.

Take first the most important or heavier aspects for the total content, which in our case would be the keywords; and later, take more specific information that would be the phrases that you manage to absorb during the second Reading Round.

For the painter it is exactly the same, normally the paintings take much more detail in the images located in front of the painting than in the images located in the background.

Also, as it is difficult to paint a small face in detail in the background of the painting with a brush, your brain also spends more work trying to get information only with the shallow data obtained in the first round.

Rocket science, but easy

But there is even more science behind this, which for us is simply a layering process, it really is about the same perspective with which space rockets are built.

To make it a little clearer, this is called System Engineering.

Systems engineering is a branch of engineering responsible for the design, application, programming, and maintenance of management systems.

This works mainly studying any existing system and seeks to implement optimize complex systems applying theoretically the systemic paradigm while in conjunction with other disciplines establishes the relationship between several processes and organs together, generating several results that together merge A common purpose.

A theoretical example of systems engineering is our body, while you are reading this a system completely separated from the others is responsible for pumping the blood around your body, while your respiratory system is responsible for absorbing oxygen and transform it in such a way that can be transferred to the blood.

Likewise, your cognitive system is allowing you to absorb all the information I am offering you, converting it into useful knowledge so that you can apply it later.

Each and every one of these processes is added, creating a macro system that you would come to be you.

The connection

The principle is the same, in this case, we are combining several systems of your capacity for cognitive development, to accelerate your reading speed, while radically improving your absorption of the information provided in the text.

In this way, we take advantage of the entire main system of the right hemisphere of the brain, helping you absorb information more easily, while the left hemisphere is responsible for processing information processing unconsciously, making good use of the information that you already have in memory.

How can you notice we are using three systems at the same time?

- Your visual perception

- Your memory, through the recognition of the information expressed in the symbols/words.

- Your cognitive system, which is responsible

for directly linking the visual perception of the symbols with the mental image of the object in your memory.

By doing this by phases, in the same way, in which a rocket is built, we establish a firmer basis for the management of information.

The first step of our Carousel method to speed up reading establishes the keywords as symbols which causes your brain to put itself in an alert mode with respect to the information related to those words.

Subsequently, during the second part, the following two systems are established. By obtaining blocks of words or phrases after having used your sight and activated your memory, the left hemisphere of the brain does the rest of the work connecting the loose ends and converting the basic information it has obtained into a new result, which is the final information, subconsciously analyzed as images, and more easily absorbed.

Thanks to all this process, your mind streamlines the work efficiently avoiding focusing all its processing capacity in each of the words and allowing you to observe a wider spectrum of ideas contained in the text.

As a result, you will not only read faster but you will obtain a more accurate global understanding of the information contained in each piece of text you are reading when using this method.

To sum up

The two main objectives of the Carousel method for rapid reading are: 1) not to focus directly on the text or analyze it constantly to wear down less the sight and enhance your reading speed; and 2) achieve that your brain automatically analyzes the text as an image using its previous knowledge of the language as a basis.

The skills we use through the Carousel method to reduce the time we spend on our reading without reducing understanding are the same ones that we apply in the learning process and in the creation process

The root of the problem is in education if it teaches us to analyze the symbols in combination with the words based on the ease of the visual means available, but this added an intermediate process forcing the left side of the brain to work in a conscious way.

The learning process has 2 important steps that are assimilation in which we perceive the external world and incorporate it internally, and accommodation, which is the process by which we adopt the previous knowledge we have to be compatible with the information acquired externally

The traditional process of reading, then internally consists of 3 steps, the assimilation of the text as a symbol which the word represents, the assimilation of the word in the representation of the image, and the connection of the image with its meaning.

The Carousel method works differently since it uses the right side of the brain to absorb information more quickly by replacing the perception of the text as a symbol by the perception of the text directly as an image.

As with a videotape, when we see the movement Carousel we can only see the part that we are allowed to see each time requiring a broad approach, followed by a more specific one in order to be able to evaluate exactly what we are seeing.

Having a two-step process that goes from the broad to the specific allows obtaining a more stable form of information reception and processing.

This process is called System Engineering and is applied to the creation of much more complex processes and systems such as space rockets.

The systems that play an important role when you use the Carousel method are your visual perception, your memory, and your cognitive system.

Chapter VI: Putting the carousel method to the test

For this point you already have an idea of exactly how the Carousel method works for fast reading, in addition I teach you or in a large part how the learning process really works, What is the way in which your brain is adapting the information it receives for turn it into useful knowledge, and what are the basic principles that govern and drive this method giving a formal basis for its usefulness.

Nevertheless, the theory is not everything, not even close, and it is the moment to put into practice everything you have learned throughout this book.

In this last chapter, we will devote ourselves exclusively to test everything learned through a unique exercise in which you will read one 1500-words text block applying the Carousel method, and then we will evaluate what has been your development with Regarding your usual reading time, and the result you obtained when you made the first reading of 500 words in Chapter 3.

The goal you have at this moment is to achieve reading with an acceptable level of comprehension you are 1500 words in an approximate time of 4 and a half minutes, which is exactly equivalent to 90 seconds for every 500 words.

Again, Remember that you must apply the two are basic waves that make up the Carousel method, which are:

Observing the text in a relaxed way paying attention only to the keywords, as well as the words that stand out on their own account in plain sight.

Making use of the words that you previously obtained, to visualize the text from top to bottom with a little more care, observing in more detail groups of words.

Are you ready to see how much you have improved?

THE CRYSTAL EGG

From Tales of Space and Time by H. G. Wells

Until not long ago, there was a small and dirty store near Seven Dials, in which some yellow letters and discolored by the weather read the name of -C. Cave, Naturalist, and Dealer in Antiquities-. The products he offered were strangely varied. It ranged from elephant tusks to an incomplete game of chess, a box of eyes, beads, weapons, a pair of tiger skulls and a human skull, an antique vintage cabinet, a flying mosquito, some stuffed monkeys and one of them with a lamp in his hand. Fishing accessories, an empty glass bowl, extremely dirty and something that looked like an ostrich egg. By the time this story begins, there was also a kind of crystal mass, carved in the shape of an egg and carefully polished, with particular brightness. There were two people there, looking out the window. A thin, tall cleric, and a dark-skinned young man in a discreet suit with a black beard who, speaking with anxious gesticulation, seemed nervous for his partner to buy what he had come for.

While they were still on the site, Mr. Cave entered the place, still carrying in his beard the bread and butter of his tea. His face fell in surprise when he observed these subjects and the object they would have considered to acquire. He cast a guilty look over his shoulder and gently proceeded to close the door. He was a pale man of short stature and with watery blue eyes; the dirty gray of his hair, his old-fashioned silk hat, and his ragged blue dress matched the carpet slippers under his heel. He watched them as they argued. One of the men reached into his trouser pocket, extracted some money, checked it and smiled warmly and pleasantly.

The old man had a worse look when they entered the establishment. The cleric, without giving him too much thought, asked about the price of the glass egg. Cave looked toward the door that led to the living room and then exclaimed in a passive tone of voice that the price would be five pounds. The cleric told him in protest that the price was high, speaking neutrally, both to his companion, as Mr. Cave did; in fact, that price was much higher than what Cave had in mind when exhibiting the glass egg, and somehow they tried to negotiate that value. Mr. Cave went to the door of the shop and held it open with one hand. -Five pounds is the price,- he explained as if he wanted to avoid the hassle of unprofitable negotiation. While doing this, the upper part of a female face appeared on the glass of the door that led to the living room, who looked curiously at the two -buyers-. -Five pounds is the price,- Cave exclaimed in a firmer tone.

-Pay the five pounds- exclaimed the dark-haired young man, his partner, who until now remained expectant, avoiding participating in the conversation. The cleric looked back at him, in an attempt to denote if the young man was being

serious, and when he looked back at Cave, he realized that his face was blank. -It's a lot of money,- the cleric said as he reached into his pocket trying to figure out whether or not he had more resources. He would have little more than thirty shillings, so he went to his partner, with whom he shared a considerable level of confidence. This was an opportunity for Mr. Cave to organize his thoughts better, so he began to explain nervously to his clients that the crystal they wanted was not, in effect, fully open to a sale. Both the young man and the cleric were amazed by this fact, as expected, and asked him why he did not say this before giving a price for the object. The old man was confused, but he stuck firmly to his story, the crystal was not for sale that afternoon as a probable buyer had already appeared. Both men were skeptical of this, for them, this was little more than an attempt to raise the price further, so they made it look like they were leaving the store. However, just at that moment, the door of the room opened and the owner of the silhouette and the eyes that were observed by the glass of the door made an appearance.

It was a young woman of great size and crude features, much more corpulent than Mr. Cave; the woman walked in a heavy way as she approached the men with a flushed face. -The crystal is for sale,- he exclaimed. -And five pounds is a sufficient price for this object. I have no idea what the problem is Cave, why not accept this man's offer? -

The old man, quite disturbed by the interruption, looked at the woman over the edge of his glasses and, with anger and without showing too much security, affirmed his right to manage his business as he pleased. Then a conflict began. The two men stopped their step and watched the funny scene interested, offering support at one time to Mr. Cave's wife with some suggestion. The administrator, meanwhile, led the discussion clinging to an absurd and impossible story that there was an investigator interested in the crystal for that morning, and his insistence became a problem. But he clanged insistently to his point until the dark-haired young man managed to put an end to such controversy. The young man's proposal was simple, they would call back after two days, to give a fair chance to the supposed investigator. -And then, we insist- the cleric explained, -Five pounds.- Ms. Cave apologized on behalf of her husband, and told them that sometimes it was "a bit strange". Once the cleric and the boy had retired, the couple began with a "free" discussion of the incident, in all its aspects.

The lady spoke with Cave in a firm and frank manner. The man was at a crossroads, trembling because of the mixture of emotions and confused among his various stories; affirming on the one hand that another customer was interested in the said object, and on the other that such a crystal could really be worth ten guineas. -Then why did you ask for five pounds? - Asked his wife. -Let me run my business my way! - Replied the man.

Together with them, his stepson and stepdaughter also lived, and at dinner that night the controversial negotiation was again discussed. None of them thought that Mr. Cave's negotiation methods were highly efficient, and his actions seemed, above all, really crazy.

-It's my opinion that he has refused to sell that crystal before- said his stepson, a stupid eighteen-year-old boy.

-But five pounds! - exclaimed the stepdaughter, a twenty-six-year-old argumentative girl.

Mr. Cave's answers lacked argument and solidity; He could only affirm in whispers that he knew what was best for his business. He was taken from the table without having finished eating at the store, to close it at night with his ears on fire and his eyes full of tears for the inconvenience. -Why had he left the glass in the display case for so long? That problem was haunting him at that moment. By then, he could not think of a way to avoid the sale.

After dinner, the young people got ready and left the table, as did his wife, who went up to analyze in more detail the commercial aspects of the glass with a little sugar, lemon and others in hot water. The old man entered the shop and stayed there until late, apparently, to prepare decorative pebbles for the goldfish antiques, but, this was not really his purpose, yet something that will be better explained later. The next day, the woman entered the store and realized that the glass had been removed from the stained glass counter and placed carefully behind some books used on angling. The woman moved the relic to a visible position. But she did not discuss the matter anymore since a headache was enough for a single debate. Mr. Cave was always discouraged, so he spent a very unpleasant day, more distracted than he usually was, and most of all irritable. In the afternoon, when his wife took her usual nap, the man withdrew the glass from the window again.

The next day, Cave had to deliver an order for

canine fish at a school near the hospital, where they would be used to do dissecting exercises. While the man was not there, the mind of the lady returned to the subject of the crystal, and the expenses that could do thanks to an unexpected gain of five pounds. She already had some ideas in mind, among others, a green silk dress for her and maybe a trip to Richmond, when the front doorbell rang loudly inviting her to go to the store. It was an exam coach who came to complain about a missing delivery, some frogs that had to be ready for dissection requested the day before. Personally, the lady did not agree with this branch of her husband's business, and the client, who had explained the incident in a rather aggressive tone, withdrew after a short exchange of words, totally polite, from his perspective. While in the shop, Mrs. Cave's gaze was naturally in search of the glass egg, after all this was her guarantee of five pounds and a few dreams fulfilled. What would be her surprise when she realized that she was no longer there?

The woman went to look for it where she found it hidden the previous day in the lockers. But it was not there, so she began anxiously searching for the entire store.

When the man returned after closing his dogfish business, it was about two forty-five in the afternoon. Cave found his shop extremely messy and his wife stressed, upset and kneeling behind the counter. The man's face looked hot and angry when the doorbell signaled his return and the woman immediately accused him of "hiding" it. (Wells, 2013)

You felt the difference, right?

Well, it's not just a matter of feeling it, if you took the time correctly, you should have taken approximately 4 minutes and 30 seconds to read the entire text. It is also sure that you have fully understood what reading is about.

Now **if you managed that your stopwatch mark around 3 minutes, congratulations!**

This means that you have achieved an incredible breakthrough by reducing your reading time at a rate of 500 words per minute.

On the other hand, **if you did not achieve a mark close to 4 minutes and a half, do not worry**, depending on what your initial time was, I'm sure you've seen a quite remarkable improvement with respect to your reading speed.

In addition, everything is really a matter of practice, it took me a couple of weeks to reach the 500 words per minute.

As we have shown throughout this book the Carousel method is really a way to simplify the internal process to which your brain is subjected when you undertake a reading.

With this last exercise, you must have managed to observe a quite drastic improvement with respect to the moment in which you started to read the book, and you are ready to make your performance improve through practice.

Practice is everything

Continuing with the previous point, the Carousel method makes initial use of the simple functions of the right hemisphere of the brain, this means that with enough practice you can achieve an improvement as drastic as 500 words per minute

However, it is also necessary that you apply this method frequently, to accustom your brain to automatically take the corresponding processes and obtain results that last over time.

Do not worry if at first you find it a bit difficult, if you are a person who is used to analyzing absolutely all the information that is absorbed is likely to find some obstacles in the way, but I do practice this method at least once a day for a while, Even if you do it Only with small blocks of text, you will notice improvements in a matter of days.

Also, if unlike me, you are not being bombarded with overwhelming amounts of text to study or you need a more practical guide to achieve your goals, stay tuned.

Soon I will be publishing content methods to practice this method, designed in order to achieve results quickly and efficiently.

Know your numbers

If you lack time for reading or you have trouble understanding what you read, the carousel method is an amazing tool to make a change.

But in order to know if you are really improving, it is important for you to know how fast you are actually going.

The average reading speed varies, but **a slow reader usually takes a minute to read a maximum of 100 words**.

The average speed of an adult in Europe and America **is around 200 words** and **great readers, usually go for around 400 words per minute**.

If you managed to reach a rate of 500 words per minute when doing the previous exercise, that means you could read a book like "Moby Dick" in just seven hours. *–In other words, you are now way above average.*

But, how fast can you really go?

Despite the opinion of some experts, the world record for rapid reading is 4700 words per minute.

Although it is clearly a very isolated case, with the right training, any regular Joe you could get to read around 750 words per minute.

Additional tools to boost your reading speed

At this point, I'm going to share with you some extra tips and techniques that are compatible with the carousel method for fast reading, and which will ensure that you go way further in much less time:

Look for blocks instead of words

To read we are moving the focus of our sight from one word to another. This eye movement is called saccadic.

The detail with this is that sometimes the new word we are looking to focus on is not entirely focused on the fovea, and this reduces our ability to recognize it immediately.

Some quick reading methods recommend pre-adjusting or previewing the next word while reading each one, which requires a lot of practice time and high levels of concentration.

However, this may be predictable in other ways, one of which is observing the words as a box, a technique that you can apply during the second step of the Carousel method.

Read as you speak

Another technique that you can combine with the Carousel method to facilitate the speed of reading, is to maintain a reading rate equivalent to the speed with which you normally emit your words.

To do this you have to put aside that you gave us at the beginning of stop vocalizing what you read, because on the opposite side you will complete the information you do not know in your mind trying to do it at the same speed at which you do when you speak, that is, you are going to think as if it is you who is emitting the information instead of receiving it.

The good writer is the best reader

According to Sally Andrews, an expert in cognitive psychology at the University of Sydney, people who have better handling of spelling and grammar tend to assimilate information more efficiently.

The reason for this, although you do not believe it, we explained earlier in the book.

The more words that are stored in your memory correctly, the easier it is for your brain to assimilate its meaning and see them as images.

Get in shape

Although it seems incredible your health plays a fundamental role in your reading ability.

The better your physical condition, the longer you will be able to support focused on an accurate reading.

Additionally, the better your cardiovascular capacity, your brain will be better oxygenated which helps it to work more efficiently.

Train your memory

When you have free time exercised also your memory, how we explained earlier in the fifth chapter your memory is one of the three systems that underlies the whole process of rapid reading of the method of Carousel.

In other words, the better your retention capacity, the easier it will be to apply this technique.

Do not stay alone

Attend fast-reading groups, or create groups with friends. Among other things, the reason for this is to promote a healthy competition environment, which will greatly help you to improve quickly through mutual support and comparison.

Never look back

Once you have finished the second phase of the Carousel method, avoid reading the same block of text again.

Unconsciously most people reread the text that they have finished halfway through the goal, delaying reading speed up to 30%, for this reason, it is important to establish clear reading goals, either half a page or a full page at a time when applying the Carousel method, and do not look back once you have finished with each goal.

Always go further

Learning to read quickly has many more benefits than simply accumulating some extra time by finishing the study texts beforehand.

So do not for a moment think that the application of the carousel method for quick reading will be something that you will only use while you are in college.

Among other things, There are certain aspects of daily life in which knowing how to read quickly while maintaining an adequate understanding will make things much easier.

- Never stay behind! You can keep up with your subscriptions to magazines and blogs and newspapers as well as a multitude of web pages that currently always have news that may be of interest to improve your professional life.

- Without having to sacrifice more free time you can dedicate yourself to reading all the best sellers that may interest you, as well as keeping up with the trends of both fiction books and Non-Fiction books.

- To read and capture information quickly you will also have the opportunity to become expert in other areas in short periods of time. This way when there is something you do not know, you simply have to search and read about it to have a good idea about what you need to learn.

- Read and keep growing at all times, having the skills to read quickly and without physical exhaustion, you can also spend less time acquiring new skills or looking for new forms of personal development.

- Through reading you can discover hundreds of new worlds, and connect with hundreds of new people, so the ability you are acquiring through this book to use the Carousel method to streamline your reading time will be useful throughout of your life.

As we indicated earlier, practice is everything, so in the end, it is you who must take the tools and use this new process to obtain new knowledge.

While there are new books at your fingertips or newly written information around you, your possibilities are unlimited.

To sum up

By implementing the carousel method to read quickly you must have noticed an improvement.

If you managed to read the text of 1,500 words in 3 minutes or less, you have achieved an incredible advance.

If you were able to read the 1500 word text in approximately 4 and a half minutes, it means that you have advanced according to what we established with the method at the beginning and it is certain that you will be able to make your reading even faster in the future.

If you did not manage to read the entire text block in less than 4 and a half minutes, do not worry, mastering the right side of your brain is not necessarily something you achieve at first and with some practice, you will start to see more progress.

It is important that you keep yourself in practice so that the effect of this method is sustainable.

If you prefer to work with guided practices, keep in mind that I will be publishing books with practical exercises.

Conclusion

When you reach this point you should have grown a lot with respect to the speed of reading and knowledge about the functioning of your cognitive abilities compared to when you started reading this book.

Throughout these pages you have had the opportunity to see the reasons and motivations that led me to create the Carousel method, as well as that moment in which the idea came to me suddenly and as the principles of absorption and management of the information, and efficiency, took part in the creation of a quick reading method that you can only apply with reading in this book.

In addition to this, I have provided you with the basic knowledge necessary to understand exactly the way in which your learning process work, as well as the information necessary, to understand the brain functions that are doing the hard work when applying the Carousel method.

In this way, you are prepared to understand how your brain works and how efficiently, we take advantage of the duality of its structure and functions to streamline the efficiency of your reading process.

Thanks to the last chapter of this book you already know exactly how to apply the Carousel method and you could also show the remarkable improvements it offers with respect to reading speed.

I greatly appreciate the time to understand, analyze and process the quick reading method that I have designed for you, and likewise, I hope that this represents a substantial advantage in your life as a reader from now on.

Remember to keep practicing, so that the benefit of this method is sustainable over time since the processing of the text as an image instead of as a symbol is something that goes against the standards that have been imposed from small to mid-educational levels.

If you want your practices to be guided stay tuned as I will be offering more standardized exercises and content soon.

Change your life

Most people see reading as a free-time luxury, but the reality is that by keeping this method in practice and making sure you read constantly to nurture your abilities you can achieve much more in your personal and professional life, in much less time.

Agatha Christie read 200 books a year, meanwhile, the founder of Facebook, Mark Zuckerberg, finishes a book every two weeks.

It is a well-known fact that Theodore Roosevelt read a book a day, and sometimes more.

However, distracted by the audiovisual media, sports, and trends in social networks, it seems that it is increasingly difficult for us to open a space of our time to reading, but believe me, reading a book from time to time can impel you towards a better future.

John Sutherland, author, columnist and professor emeritus of Modern English Literature at UCL University in London says he has read 150 books during 2015.

Just like these characters, there are hundreds of people who have achieved much more in their lives just by allowing themselves to incorporate constant reading as part of their day to day activities, and you now have the tools to start working on a better future.

Leave a few minutes a day to play with your quick reading, undertake new trips and acquire new knowledge that helps you grow.

Bibliography

Arthur Conan Doyle, S. (2017). A Scandal in Bohemia (1st Ed.). La Vergne: Dreamscape Media.

Levy-Agresti, J. & Sperry, R. W. Differential perceptual capacities in major and minor hemispheres. Proc. Nat. Acad. Sci., 1968, 61, 1151.

Piaget, J. (1936). Origins of intelligence in the child. London: Routledge & Kegan Paul.

Roger Wolcott Sperry. (1974) Lateral specialization in the surgically separated hemispheres. F. Schmitt and F. Worden (Eds.), Third Neurosciences Study Program (Cambridge: MIT Press) 3: 5-19

Wells, H. (2013). *Tales of space and time* (1st ed.). Lanham: Start Classics.